HOW TO CATCH A UNICORN

Or

A SURE-FIRE WAY TO BUILD YOUR

Private Practice Team

Find the Confidence You Need to Supervise Postgraduate
Psychology Interns and Build the Team You Deserve

Dr Tess Crawley

Clinical & Forensic Psychologist
Mentor to Mental Health Professionals
Director, Dr Tess Crawley & Associates

CONTENTS

It took me a little while to come around to writing this book. It's a topic I'm frequently asked about. Initially I was surprised that other psychologists were so interested in this concept. I've successfully hosted provisional psychologists in my private practice for over 10 years, mostly as postgraduate clinical psychology interns. I didn't realise it was so unusual. But apparently so, and so here we. I'm happy to share what I've learnt along the way.

Before we begin, a side note. This book is written from an Australian point of view. But aside from geographical specifics around training and registration, I hope the spirit of this book will have a universal appeal. The aim is to encourage you to find the confidence to take on a student within your practice with the added benefit of safely and confidently building your team as you go.

So far, the process of writing has been a bit of an eye-opener for me. It has led me to reflect on my own experiences of receiving supervision, especially as a student back in the day. I commenced my postgraduate clinical psychology training in 1999. Things have certainly changed a bit since then.

My first placement was pretty ramshackle, I have to admit. Before the days of Medicare, before AHPRA, even before any kind of reliable internet, it seems the world swung a little looser. I was recruited into my first placement by a fellow student who was snowed under by the case load at our University Psychology Clinic. Fearless, I dived in, despite the rather hands-off *"you'll be right"* supervision we received at the time. My very first client (ever!) told me he was suicidal. My second client handed me a note from his GP asking me to assist with erectile dysfunction. Holy Monkey! It could only get better from there.

I coped, doing the best I could. In hindsight I'm horrified by all the things that could have gone horribly wrong (but thankfully didn't). At the time I was so conscientious, so keen, and so scared of doing the wrong thing, that nothing (it seemed) was going to slip through my net. And that's the greatest thing about students, their energy!

Subsequent placements were more organised (mostly). At least I had regular supervision. And what amazing supervisors I had! I still use some of my old supervisors' gems to help my own supervisees. There are things my interns hear from me that come directly from the mouths of my supervisors ... *"Don't write essays in the case notes!"* being but one example.

I've had supervisors who were quiet and gentle, supervisors who were ball-breakingly blunt, and others who were completely disorganised but clinically brilliant. They all had something to share with me. Their experience, their knowledge, their support. On reflection, what mattered most was knowing I wasn't on my own. The best supervisors listened. And asked great questions.

Now that I think about it, that was the greatest tool my supervisors gave me, lots of questions. By being curious, my supervisors taught me to see what gaps I had in my knowledge of a certain client. They taught me that no-one knows all the information at once, and that I need to continue my assessment of clients as I go (because things change, who'd have thought!). By asking me questions about my clients, they weren't trying to point out that I'd missed something in my assessment (as I initially feared), they were demonstrating genuine interest. They were curious. And they demonstrated that if I didn't know the answer now, I could find it out. No big deal.

These days I'm an experienced supervisor, sure. But I'm no guru. And I'm not interested to train you in the rules and regulations of supervision. That's what the formal AHPRA-approved supervisor training workshops are for. But I do know how to build trust in the supervisor/supervisee relationship. I do know that it's daunting when you start supervising (hello, imposter fears!). I know that some students will appear confident but actually be terrified. Others will seem anxious but are brilliant with clients. And I do know that you're a better supervisor than you give yourself credit for.

In some capacity or other, I've supervised over 50 interns and provisional psychologists over the years, not to mention all the clinical registrars, senior level psychologists, and other supervisors that I've also provided supervision and mentoring to. And I've been at the receiving end of supervision ranging from the woeful to literally world-

How to Catch a Unicorn

leader level (an absolute highlight). I've been very lucky in my career. I was taught very early on (from a supervisor) that we never stop needing support as professionals. We never know all the answers, and we will always need to ask lots of questions.

I hope you'll find some of what I have to say here helpful. I hope it will lead you on your way to confidently incorporating psychology interns into your private practice, first as students and then as valued team members.

CHAPTER 1

BEING SUPERVISED

When I was a student, clinical placements were fairly adhoc. At least that's how it seemed to me at the time. Our placement coordinator was a full-time lecturer who bravely tried to manage the placement program off the side of his desk. Let's just say he did his best.

My first placement was in the University Psychology Clinic. I was recruited by a fellow student and supervision was fairly informal and infrequent, offered on an as-needs basis. I received no formal induction into how the clinic worked, other than from my fellow student. She and I were often in the clinic alone. I hadn't even finished my first semester of postgraduate clinical training, which we had been told was a prerequisite for doing any placements at all. In other words, I was completely and utterly under-trained and unprepared for those very vulnerable people whose care was placed into my hands. The only thing going in their favour was that I was a mature-age student with a bit of life experience under

How to Catch a Unicorn

my belt, coupled with some basic training in CBT. I fumbled my way through, doing the best job I could. In hindsight I think I did okay.

During my ad hoc placement career, I organised a placement for myself due to a lack of available child placements at the time (an essential component of the postgraduate clinical psychology program). I created a new placement opportunity with a local charity where I supported teenagers and slightly younger children as they navigated the choppy waters of watching a family member's experience of cancer. It wasn't a particularly challenging role and it wasn't a particularly clinical role, but it was the first time I'd had much to do with young people in distress and I found it thoroughly satisfying, if somewhat emotionally challenging at times. That placement would never pass muster these days, as there was no supervision on-site. But I convinced someone to supervise me through that placement in an off-site capacity, and it went well. I was always one to create roles where none existed (in a former life as an out-of-work-actor, two friends and I created our own theatre company to create our own work – unpaid of course, but fulfilling nonetheless). But I was also careful to not be seen as a "cowboy", going off on a tangent outside the boundaries of my training. I still value initiative in students when I see it, but remain watchful of cowboys. That conflict between confidence and competence worries me no end!

Towards the end of my program I did a placement in a private hospital's psychiatric ward under the supervision of a fabulous clinical psychologist. She was forthright, and talked to me about being strong, clear, and decisive in my clinical work. This was my first experience of working alongside a supervisor in a placement. Just the luxury of observing her with clients was an amazing learning opportunity. I learned a lot from her about the interpersonal dynamics of therapy, and how to tailor that to meet the client on their level. She also taught me to be an efficient psychologist. I think *efficiency* is a word that's not used often enough in training psychologists. We are taught to document, document, document and prepare, prepare, prepare. And it's absolutely right that we learn these skills, to ensure that we're doing the best job possible. But we also need to be able to put these skills in our back pocket sometimes. We need to learn how to fly by the seat of our pants when necessary, how to "break the rules" appropriately, how to know when a grey area ethically is safe enough to step into.

I think one of the biggest things that students are left with when they leave university is the need to write down every word that comes out of the client's mouth and every thought that comes into their own mind with regards to that client. After what I learned on placement about efficiency, I still find myself regularly telling my own students to *"stop writing essays"* in case notes.

So, what do students want from their supervisors? Based on what I learned as a supervisee, coupled with what I've learned as a placement coordinator and a supervisor myself, there are three main elements to what students value most from supervisors. The rest is window dressing.

What Students Want From A Supervisor

Competence

Students want to know that you know what you're doing. The best way for them to know this is to watch you doing it. Let them observe you. It might feel awkward initially, but you'll just have to get over yourself. Trust me.

How to Catch a Unicorn

Confidence

Students need for you to have a quiet confidence in your own abilities, and in their abilities too. Confidence in each other is built on rapport, trust, and great communication. Lead them into situations that build and stretch their confidence. Don't leave them hanging, scarred for life in dangerous situations, as has happened to me. (I completed my final placement in a prison setting, after which the university deemed it an unsafe environment for students. More on that story another time.)

Collegiality

Students want to know that you value their ideas and opinions, that you consider them a colleague, and that you'll guide them safely into the profession they've been working so hard to enter. Be kind. Always. And buy them coffee sometimes. They're poor.

CHAPTER 2

HOW I BECAME A SUPERVISOR

These days becoming a supervisor requires a bit of conscious effort, at least if you want to be a Board Approved Supervisor. Don't worry, I'm not going to go through all that palaver here, there are plenty of training opportunities through the APS and elsewhere where you can read the thing, do the thing, video the thing, and then hey presto! You're a supervisor.

Sorry if I sound like I'm making light of what is these days a very arduous and deliberate process. I completely agree that there should be formal training for supervisors, and that standards of supervision need to be maintained. (But does it HAVE to be so boring? … But I digress.)

I became a supervisor *"in the olden days"*, as my kids would say. As I was transitioning from my PhD into a lecturer role, I began to take on research students. Initially I was supervising Graduate Diploma students' very small-scale research projects. In fact, one of those supervisees has recently

How to Catch a Unicorn

joined my practice as a fully-fledged psychologist after years of further study elsewhere. I then moved on to supervising Honours students. And when those students were accepted into the MPsych and DPsych programs, they wanted me to supervise them again. As if by magic I suddenly found myself supervising my very own research team, The Clinical Forensic Psychology Lab at the University of Tasmania. We studied lots of fascinating things as a team – Psychopathic personality traits; aggression in women; and distinguishing accident from suicide in single vehicle fatalities. All of my research team members were postgraduate clinical psychology students. They all wanted to be practicing psychologists when they graduated.

As I had a private practice on the side, it seemed obvious for them to want to do a placement with me when the time came.

And so, suddenly I found myself hosting interns in what was then a solo private practice.

Nobody taught me anything about supervision. I only had my own supervisors to rely on for guidance. I had been a registered psychologist for three or four years by then, but hadn't gotten around to jumping through the hoops for membership (now called Fellowship) of the APS Clinical College. Remember, this was before the days of AHPRA and Areas of Endorsement. Back then, the only formal way to call yourself a Clinical Psychologist was to become a College member (or eligibility for same). So I asked my old ball-breaker supervisor if she would supervise me through my period of supervised practice to gain College membership – which she graciously agreed to do in exchange for coffee. Bless her.

So, my first interns benefitted from (a) a prior working relationship with me, which made it easy for us to trust each other in the therapy setting; (b) my enthusiasm for being new to the game; and (c) vicarious supervision through me from my own very-experienced and very-unafraid-to-say-it-like-it-is-supervisor. What could possibly go wrong?

Nothing. I can proudly say I'm still on speaking terms with all of them, and over the years many of my interns have stayed on to be members of my private practice team.

But I'm jumping ahead. Again.

CHAPTER 3

BUT I DON'T HAVE TIME TO SUPERVISE INTERNS!

Here's the rub. Postgraduate students require one hour of supervision per day of placement. I can hear your cries of *"lost income"* from here! Stop it and listen for a minute.

Now if you think of that as having to set aside an hour every day that they are with you, you'll balk. I know you will. Everyone does. And that is why so few private practices host postgraduate interns. Mistake. Big mistake. If you want to expand your team, that is. If you're happy being on your own in your practice seeing client after client after client with no lunch break, all power to you. But then why are you reading this book?

An hour every day? You'll think *"but that's a whole client I'm missing out on"* or *"I'm booked solid for the next eight weeks"* or *"I don't wanna"*. But that's just your time scarcity mindset in action. (Haven't heard of time scarcity mindset? Google it.

Or better yet, join one of my mentoring programs where I'll help you overcome it.) Basically, you're *afraid* that you don't have enough time. But you do. I promise.

I know this to be true, because supervision is made up of a bunch of activities. Obviously sitting together face-to-face having intense case discussions is one of those activities. But did you know that having the student observe you – or you observing the student – is also counted as supervision? Did you know you can break the hour-long case discussion into shorter increments across the course of the day? If you get to thinking about all the ways you and your intern could spend time together discussing their work, discussing their case load, discussing testing materials, diagnostic dilemmas, ethical dilemmas, and so on, you'll find the same thing I did: Students will walk away from your placement with MORE supervision hours than they need. And you won't be bankrupted in the process.

But before we go on, let's be clear here. When I say interns, I'm talking about postgraduate students (typically clinical psychology in my experience, but not limited to that area of practice) who are in a traditional six-year coursework-plus-placement Masters program or higher. I will speak about 5+1 and 4+2 internships in a later chapter. They're a completely different beast and have additional considerations if the internship is to be successful for them and for you.

The Power of Observation

Time and again students in my practice talk about how much they gain from observing other clinicians. I have a group practice now, and my team members are all welcoming of interns observing them (as long as clients are happy with

How to Catch a Unicorn

the idea, of course). But even when I was a sole practitioner, interns on placement with me would observe my sessions, take additional notes, and ask LOTS of questions after the end of the session. Sometimes, as their confidence grew, they would ask questions of the client in-session. Over time of course they build the confidence to take over sessions if appropriate. But I'll talk more about that in later chapters.

In my mind, the best thing about students having the opportunity to observe experienced clinicians in action is that they soon learn that there are several ways to skin a cat. As a student they are typically taught that there is ONE way to treat anxiety, for example (manualised CBT). But when they watch the seasoned professionals in action, they see how we have each moulded our training to suit our own personal style. We all come from the same basis of evidence-based practice, but our own flavour leads to an infinite variety of roads that therapy might take to reach the same positive outcome. I have often wondered if I'd be burned at the stake for saying things like this, but so far so good.

Phone, online, email supervision

I have kids and so I only work school hours. My practice is busy, with multiple clinicians in the office at any given time. Students rarely find themselves in the practice without another clinician present, and of course we always have admin on hand as well for added support and safety. But I just can't physically be there ALL the time. So, I add a mix of phone calls, emails, and online platforms such as Zoom for additional 'face-to-face' contact. Again, these elements of supervision contribute to the hour-per-day-placement supervision load and also keep the interns feeling supported and secure knowing that help is just at the end of the phone.

Of course, I also have the luxury of having additional approved supervisors on site, but don't let that throw you.

Case notes, reports, and letters

It seems fairly obvious that we would need to co-sign any letters and reports written by the intern. Not that there are likely to be very many of those. However, it is also vital that you are monitoring how your intern is going with their case notes. Are they keeping them up-to-date? Are they falling behind (they'd better not!) Are they demonstrating the necessary competencies? Are they writing "essays"?

To be truthful with you, this is the most time-consuming task — reviewing and signing off on case notes. But it is necessary, and it is a task you can do at home after the kids are asleep (or you can delegate, which I'll get to later).

Remember, one of the things interns need to learn is to be efficient. They need to be efficient with their time so they stay on track with their tasks and stay on time for their clients. And to achieve this, they need to be efficient with their notes. They also need to be efficient with your time. They will learn to grab five minutes here and there to run an idea or a question by you while you're on the way to the loo. They will learn to be prepared ahead of their supervision meetings. Coach them to be efficient. (Oh, and try to model efficiency yourself — what are your case notes like? Are you prepared for meetings?)

We have a fairly simple rule in my practice — 50 minutes with the clients, 10 minutes to write the notes. I said it was simple. I didn't say it was easy. Interns and graduates seem to struggle with conciseness. They are taught to over-document. They take copious handwritten notes in session and then want to transcribe them verbatim into the file.

How to Catch a Unicorn

They are scared to leave anything out in case it's important. They are terrified of going before the coroner and being found lacking.

In my practice we type notes straight into our online practice management system. I discourage double note taking (handwriting and then transcribing), but I find this to be a losing battle – but I'm still fighting it! I'm all for assistive technologies, whether that be dictation tools or handwriting-to-text apps. Whatever speeds up the process but is secure and confidential as well.

Having an online practice management system is especially cool, because it means that I can review intern case notes from home, the coffee shop, or while the kids are at gymnastics. I don't need to lug heavy files home (I always used to worry I'd be THAT psychologist whose car got stolen with a boot load of files). I can read the case notes and leave a file note to state that I've seen and approved them. Done.

But guess what else? You don't have to do it all yourself.

Delegate

The intern can have a secondary supervisor who can assist with the provision of their supervision. That could be someone internal to your practice, someone from the university clinic, or someone else entirely.

For some ideas, here's how we've mixed it up in the past. With either myself or one of my other clinical psychologists as primary supervisor, a number of my interns have had one or a number of the following secondary supervisor options also in place:

> One of my team members acting as secondary supervisor responsible for checking / signing case notes;

> One of my team members providing back up support and ad hoc supervision as needed;

> An external supervisor from a previous placement happy to provide added support

> A university clinic supervisor willing to supervise a specific task that is outside my scope but a great learning opportunity for the student (e.g., educational assessments)

> A university clinic supervisor providing group supervision and/or secondary supervision

> In-house group supervision

See? Suddenly that one hour per day of placement is shaping up to be a walk in the park (literally, if you like). You don't need to do it all in one bite, or all by yourself. Be creative. Just make sure whatever you arrange is documented in the placement contract and given the thumbs up by the university.

CHAPTER 4

THE PLACEMENT COORDINATOR IS KING

The key to hosting a successful placement program within your practice is a rock solid relationship with the University Placement Coordinator. This person knows the entire pool of postgraduate students, what level of experience they've had, their personality quirks, their potential. It is your job to ensure that the Placement Coordinator has a really clear understanding of what you expect from a student on placement within the context of your unique practice.

What should you look for in an intern?

Not sure what you should expect from an intern? That's okay, here's a list of my key must-haves. I'm sure you could add to it.

1. Interns in private practice should be experienced with 1:1 client work in previous placements;

2.   Interns should be at the tail end (not the beginning) of their placement program;

3.   Interns MUST have completed at least some of their Ethics and Professional Practice training. [They need to be really clear on boundaries, how to recognise an ethical dilemma, etc.];

4.   Interns must be able to clearly identify the limits of their role (and be able to say no if asked to step outside those limits);

5.   Interns must be teachable. [Sounds obvious, I know, but you'd be surprised.]

6.   Interns should be a good fit for your team culture;

7.   Interns should have an interest in your niche practice area(s);

8.   Gold standard: Interns should be ready for full registration as soon as they finish their placement with you.

If you have a good relationship with the Placement Coordinator, and they have a good understanding of how your practice functions, most of these points will be assumed, because the Placement Coordinator will have hand-picked a student perfectly suited to your practice. That's the general idea, anyway.

How Do I Get Started?

I'm glad you asked. The first thing to do is find out who is the Placement Coordinator at your local university psychology department. They are always keen to have new placement opportunities for their students, so don't be shy about getting in touch. Let them know about your practice, your supervisor status, and what opportunities you see students having in your practice. You can do this in an email and follow up with a phone call. I'd then arrange a meeting, preferably at your practice so they can see your facility. Be magnanimous, shout them coffee!

What Should I Be Offering On Placement?

Basically, lots of client contact and lots of supervision. As I've already discussed, finding time for lots of supervision isn't really as hard as you'd imagine. I'll talk about how interns are involved in my practice in more detail in the next chapter, but for now I'd like you to stop thinking about using interns to lighten your administrative workload. I mean it. Interns are not in your practice to do your filing and photocopying. Sorry, but this is something I hear a lot. *"Can I get an intern to do admin for me?"* No. *"Can the intern do my marketing for me?"* No. *"Can an intern sit at reception?"* No. *"Can I get an intern to update our procedure manuals?"* NO!

Well, alright, I'm being a bit harsh and a bit cheeky. Of course, an intern can be *involved* in all those activities, but you need to eradicate any thought that these activities will form a major part of the placement for postgraduate students. Firstly, it does not teach them to be clinicians, and that's what they're there for. Secondly, they are not free labour. By all means employ psych students to be an administrative assistant for you. I've had wonderful success with this. But you'll be better off looking to undergraduates for this task – from Honours onwards they just don't have the time to commit to your office needs. Undergraduate psychology students are often looking for work experience in psychology practices, you might consider a volunteer work experience program, with an option for successful volunteers to become employed administrative team members. But I digress …

Think about your practice focus. Are you a predominantly child and family practice? Great, you can offer a child placement. Are you a forensic practice? Great opportunity for an intern to learn about assessment, the balance between psychology and law, and how to handle legal requests. Remember, APAC-approved courses require students to complete a certain range of components within their placement program. You don't need to address all of those in the placement you're offering, but if you have a niche that isn't offered elsewhere you might find that your placement becomes a popular choice. For example, my practice sees all comers, but we have a strong perinatal focus. This means our interns have the opportunity to see clients from across the entire lifespan, from newborns through to older adults. Our placements are popular among students with a special interest in perinatal and infant mental health, and also those interested in child psychology. And because we always manage to send interns away with more client contact hours and supervision hours than they need, we're a great option for students low on hours towards the end of their placement program.

Just as you would consider your niche area when marketing to GPs for referrals, think about the same when "marketing" your practice to students looking for placements. Of course, you're not marketing directly to the students, but you are hoping for great word of mouth from both the Placement Coordinator and students who have completed placements with you.

CHAPTER 5

INTERNS ON THE LOOSE

So, you've been offered an intern. Now what? First, don't panic. I know you've got a million questions and a raging impostor scenario playing out in your mind. Breathe. You'll be fine. And you'll be supported in your role.

The placement coordinator will discuss with you the student they have in mind for you. Ask lots of questions, I've had to say no once or twice to students who were too inexperienced to suit our needs (i.e., they'd need too much "teaching" in addition to supervision). Assuming you're happy with the sound of this student, the placement coordinator will then want to arrange a pre-placement meeting with you and the intern. This is a meet-and-greet session and an opportunity for you and the intern to ask lots of questions of each other. And don't worry, you can still say no at this stage.

The placement coordinator will have a placement contract for you to sign if you're happy to proceed. This might include goals for the placement, any pre-reading you'd like the intern to complete, commencement and completion dates, number of placement days, supervision arrangements, etc. Some simple goals that I include are:

> Learn how to practice psychology within a private practice setting;

> Provide support for clients of the clinical team;

> Work collaboratively with the admin team;

> Learn to identify the limits of private practice (i.e., learning which referrals are not suited to management within a private practice setting);

> Gain experience with perinatal and infant clients;

> Develop skills in online delivery of therapy.

And so on. I'm sure you'll think of more goals specific to your practice.

Respecting the Limits of the Student Role

Another key factor that you'll want to monitor, even if you don't add it to your contract, is for the intern to know and respect the limits of their role as a student. This means that they know when to say no to admin requests and client referrals outside their scope; who to keep informed when there are changes with a client they've been working with; and when to ask questions. Of course, you need to monitor your own respect of the student role too. As the intern becomes increasingly competent and confident it is easy to forget sometimes that they're a student. (Although when you find

How to Catch a Unicorn

yourself forgetting, this is a great indicator that you're feeling that this intern could make a great ongoing team member.)

What can interns do?

Typically, the interns in my practice have already completed a placement at the University Psychology Clinic, with individual and group therapy experience. They have also usually completed another placement in a setting such as Child and Adolescent Mental Health. So, they come to us with a bit of experience under their belts. But we still don't tend to throw them in the deep end if we can help it. We usually start with lots of opportunity to observe while they find their feet. Once an intern is comfortable, we will engage them in a range of roles, such as the following:

> Observing clinicians with clients.

> Conducting phone-based "intake" sessions with new referrals (rather than a formal intake assessment, this is a means to quickly flesh out the GP referral and identify any risk factors and urgent support needs).

> Provide additional sessions to "stretch out" the therapy program for longer term clients at risk of exhausting their allocation of Medicare rebateable sessions. This is the main role of our interns. The primary clinician devises a program whereby the intern might see the client for six sessions of skills-based work (e.g., distress tolerance) before the client returns to the primary clinician. There are many ways this can work, from the intern managing most sessions with occasional review by the primary clinician, or the intern providing a discreet therapeutic package before handing the client back to the primary clinician.

What do clients think? Do many say no to intern sessions?

Clients are sometimes edgy about having an intern observe them in session, which is fine. We always follow the client's lead of course. But when a client is requiring longer-term care and are likely to quickly exhaust their Medicare allocation, it's not difficult for them to see the benefit of a shared care arrangement with an intern. We don't charge for intern sessions (and we don't pay student interns), so clients have nothing to lose.

What about referrers? Will this harm my reputation?

GPs understand the concept of a Teaching Clinic, which is what you are when you're regularly hosting interns in your practice. We don't accept direct referrals to interns, so clients are always primarily managed by a member of our team. GPs and clients appreciate that we are offering a free "add-on" service. I've never had a GP express concern about a client being supported by an intern.

What if it doesn't work out?

You can terminate placements early if you wish. There might be a number of reasons for this. It might be that the intern has proven unsuitable (this has never happened in my practice once a placement has started, although I have rejected a couple of students prior to commencement). It might be that your availability (and therefore capacity to supervise) has changed. It might be that it's just not a good

How to Catch a Unicorn

fit. Whatever the reason, you can end a placement early if you need to, without causing academic penalty to the intern. It is my belief that it is far better for an intern to finish a dud placement early rather than languish in something that's not a good fit for either party. Then they can move on to a better opportunity for them. And so can you.

CHAPTER 6

THE KEEPERS – TRANSITIONING FROM STUDENTS TO PROFESSIONALS

I remember the day very clearly when my supervisor pulled me aside in the nurses' station and said *"Tess, nobody has time to read an essay at handover!"* In a hospital setting or some other multidisciplinary teams, various people are writing their observations, their instructions, and their diagnoses into the same client file. Sometimes in handwritten format. Those files contain a lot of important information. Nobody wants to be wading through mountains of inconsequential commentary from the psychology student who feels it appropriate to air every thought she has on the matter before they find the instructions from the psychiatrist, for example. This I learned quickly.

Until my supervisor had the balls to pull me up on this, nobody had actually said to me *"Tess, this is what you need to STOP doing."* So I use this as an example with my students. I make sure they are very clear that while you need

How to Catch a Unicorn

to document everything related to risk, everything related to disclosure of abuse, you don't need to document everything about what the client was wearing, or how they appeared, or what they did on the weekend.

You need to make sure that what you're documenting is not overly disclosing the client's private information, especially when it's not really relevant to the therapeutic process. So, when a client is chatting about the weekend and having had some drinks at a friend's and hooking up with some fellow and feeling a bit shabby about it this morning, is it fair to document all of that? Is it relevant to say anything about that at all? It depends on the client's reasons for therapy of course. So, students need to ask themselves, if the client was sitting next to them watching them write those notes in their file, would they still write them? Would they modify their choice of words, or deem what they were going to say irrelevant? In other words, as a student they want to write EVERYTHING, because they're uncertain what is relevant. As a seasoned clinician they know what's relevant and what's superfluous.

I teach students on placement that they are in a transition between being a student and being a professional. They need to translate what they've learnt in student mode. They need to convert that knowledge and those skills and accommodate a more professional mode of practice. And a more professional mode of viewing what they do and how they do it. It takes a while for them to get their head around this.

This does not mean suddenly becoming a cowboy and going off half-cocked on their own little tangent, as some will want to do. It does not mean getting a *"she'll be right"* level of supervision either. It means that the student needs to take on a professional mindset, become streamlined, efficient, effective, and confident. And as their supervisor, it's your job to help them get there.

The frequency of your supervision sessions might shift as they begin to make this transition. Instead of being constantly camped outside your door ready for a game of 20 questions, your supervisee might become a bit harder to pin down, like you. Supervision sessions might become longer lunch breaks together talking about things in more detail. Like colleagues!

The danger here is to assume that everything is going smoothly and that you no longer need to be vigilant. Keep an eye on how they are feeling, especially as they approach the end of their placement, because this is when anxiety and impostor fears can increase for interns. The closer they come to becoming a *"real psychologist"*, the more anxious and not-ready they may feel. The opposite is worse, those who shun supervision because they're *"all good, thanks"*.

Do not mistake increased *competence* for increased *confidence*. The fact that they've got their clinical chops all sorted doesn't mean they feel like they have.

Conversely, and more importantly, do not mistake increased *confidence* for increased *competence*.

As an intern becomes more confident in their role, this can be mistaken for evidence of increased competence at a skill level. You need to keep an eye on both.

How do I know if an intern is doing well?

1. Case notes demonstrate a professional level of conciseness and efficiency (i.e., brief, to the point, and on time);
2. They have developed a busy case load of their own, with clients handed over to them by other clinicians within the team;

3. Their clients are engaged, they keep coming back and are progressing well in therapy;

4. The admin team starts to forget the intern is an intern, because they are so efficient, effective, and confident;

5. They seem like a seamless member of your team.

And, before you know it, with all going well, you've got a ready-made team member perfectly prepared to step up into your practice as a fully-fledged clinician. Ta dah!

CHAPTER 7

WHAT ABOUT 4+2s AND 5+1s?

Supervision of postgraduate students in your private practice should hopefully sound like a no-brainer now. It's not as onerous as you might have thought. Placements are for around 250 hours each, which at a couple of days a week ends up being around six months. Long enough to really get a feel of things (both the intern and you), but not so long as to become burdensome. And as I've stated, if you're offering placements to end-stage students, they're only a hair's breadth away from full registration when they finish up, making keeping them on fairly simple.

However, the other pathways to psychologist registration currently available in Australia have a much heavier internship obligation. These are the 4+2 and 5+1 pathways. Interns coming from these programs have (on average) different levels of training and experience from each other and from the six-year clinical (and other) Masters programs. I have not traditionally offered placements with these interns, but I have recently employed a couple. I'll walk you through it as best I can below.

The 4+2 Pathway to Registration

There has been much talk for decades about phasing out this pathway to registration, but as currently stands it is possible to become a registered psychologist in Australia after completion of an accredited four-year university program plus two years' supervised practice. Two-year internships are hard for four-year graduates to find, especially here in Tasmania where Masters-level training is the industry norm. So, these provisional psychologists often find themselves in aligned roles that may be incredibly supportive and skills-stretching, or they may be pushing it to get their work over the line in terms of AHPRA-approval. For the supervisor there is a lot of "teaching" needed as well as the ongoing supervision. In my personal opinion it is very difficult to find time in a private practice setting to offer the amount of support needed for these provisional psychologists, and it can become incredibly stressful for both parties as a result. If you can make it work as an internship in your setting, I applaud you and welcome your inside knowledge on how you made it work for you and your intern. The main problem is that the internship is for two years, which is a long time in private practice!

NOTE: The latest whispers are that AHPRA will allow the final intake for the 4+2 pathway in 2020, with all candidates on this pathway needing to be finished by 2025.

The 5+1 Pathway to Registration

The Master of Professional Psychology (MPP) is sometimes referred to as a "fast track" to registration. This is a misnomer, to be honest, and in my personal view a harder road than the traditional six-year program. Upon completion of the Honours / 4th year of psychology training, MPP candidates complete a fifth year, which is a one-year Masters program. It involves most of the same coursework involved in the two-year Clinical (or other endorsement area) Masters program, compacted into a single year. They are also required to complete at least one placement during this postgraduate, but the breadth and complexity of these placements do not seem to be as extensive as within the two-year Masters programs. I have had provisional psychologists who are graduates of the MPP apply for roles with me where their placement has been purely observational or purely role play. Not ideal.

Upon completion of the MPP the graduate is required to source their own one year ("aka +1") internship. This is not arranged for them by the university (as is also the case with the 4+2 pathway). Although they have more formal training than the 4+2 provisional psychologists, the 5+1 provisional psychologists often struggle to find a year-long internship. Hence my opinion that there is nothing "fast" about this track to registration.

Both of these pathways to registration have very specific obligations under AHPRA guidelines with regards to supervised practice. As provisional psychologists they require one-hour of supervision per 17 hours of employment. Provisional psychologists may not be engaged as contractors; they may only be engaged in employed (or volunteer) roles, thereby further limiting their options within private practice settings.

I'm yet to meet a provisional psychologist on one of these tracks to registration who has been prepared to complete unpaid placements (although I'm told they do exist), despite two-year Masters students completing all their placements

How to Catch a Unicorn

in an unpaid capacity (usually). These programs offer the anticipation that paid internships are readily available, which is far from the truth. So, if you are in a position to offer a paid internship to provisional psychologists following these pathways to registration, all power to you. I have employed a couple, but only within a federally-funded program. Without that funding, employing psychologists in general (let alone provisionals who do not attract Medicare rebates) becomes unsustainable in a practice of our size.

Having said all that, you might find yourself in the lucky position of finding a provisional psychologist at the tail-end of their internship program. Supervising a short-burst internship while they finish off their hours, followed soon after by full-registration, is an excellent investment of your time, akin to providing late-stage student placements.

CHAPTER 8

MAKING IT PAY

Okay, let's be brutally honest here. Private practice is not the cash cow we thought it would be when we were students.

I remember marvelling at the APS rate (below $200 when I was a student), thinking *"wow, those private practitioners make a killing"*! But as you well know, the reality is far different. Firstly, we tend to only charge the APS rates for a proportion of our work. Secondly, we have become unduly wedded to Medicare, which is a problem (and I will discuss this in more detail in this chapter). And thirdly, we have overheads. Big overheads. You can assume 50% of your revenue will be lost to costs. At least.

We are not charities, we are not funded by outside sources (usually). We are reliant wholly and solely on the client fees that we charge. As I heard it so eloquently put recently, *"we eat what we kill"*.

And for these reasons I get so angry when I hear references to "greedy practice owners", and complaints that it's "unethical" to offer unpaid internships.

Finding the money to pay a 4+2 or 5+1 internship is incredibly difficult. I can guarantee that any intern working with me for a full year or two would learn an incredible amount about being in private practice, would receive incredible (and varied) supervision from my in-house supervision team, and would receive plenty of in-house PD opportunities. They would be well-rounded professionals, ready to soar on their own wings upon completion.

My simple model is this:

1. Student interns on placement are unpaid (as is normal) and clients pay nothing to see them.

2. Provisional psychologists who have finished all MPsych coursework and placements (i.e., are only a few months from registration) may be employed as casuals, paid for the direct client work that they do. Their clients are charged out at a rate commensurate with what people pay to see local counsellors, and it is explained to clients that there is no rebate until their provisional psychologist achieves full registration and their Medicare Provider Number comes through. Upon achieving full registration these psychologists are offered the opportunity to join the practice as contractors. This model has worked quite well so far.

3. Provisional psychologists completing their 5+1 internship are employed as full-time or part-time clinicians under a federally funded project we have running in one part of our practice. Without that funding, I would not be offering those positions, and if the funding comes to an end (which it surely will at some point) I will no longer be able to offer them. That's the harsh reality. Below is the reason why.

Doing The Sums

At the time of writing, the base salary for a provisional psychologist in Australia is around $47,000 per annum. Then you need to assume 25% for on-costs, making that clinician cost you around $60,000 per year. Where does that money come from? Good question. And it is something we're still working on. But here's an indication for you.

Say your provisional is able to maintain a full-time case load, charging clients the same as a local counsellor, say $100 per client. If they average four clients a day, five days a week, for 43 weeks of the year (allowing for leave, illness, Christmas, etc), that's 860 clients per year. Charged at $100 each, that's $86,000 revenue. Less her salary, that's $26,000 per annum coming into the practice. That's $500 per week to cover the added administrative staffing needs, the added phone costs, and all the other added business expenses associated with an extra body in your office.

And you haven't even factored in your own lost revenue if you take time out of your diary to provide the necessary two hours per week of supervision that this cohort requires.

See? Even with paying clients, it is very difficult to make this cohort earn their own keep in private practice, sadly. Which is why the expectation of paid internships and free supervision results in them being shot in the foot before they've even started. A casual payment arrangement, especially a short-term one, is workable though.

The Medicare Dilemma

You are underservicing your community already. I know this because I've addressed this in my practice, which is

How to Catch a Unicorn

how I've been able to offer some casual paid work to our shorter-term provisional psychologists. I know what's holding you back. I can hear you shouting it from here! *But provisionals can't attract a Medicare rebate!* No, they can not. And their supervisors MUST NOT put through a claim to Medicare for services provided by their interns. (This is Medicare fraud. Bad things happen if you commit Medicare fraud. Very bad things.)

In order to make this work, you will need to have a serious look at your relationship with Medicare (and any other external funding source that makes up a large part of your practice). I know of some practices that are divorcing themselves from Medicare. Why? It has the potential to trap us in an unprofitable mindset. What do I mean by this?

How often do you choose (or feel pressured) to bulk bill clients? How often do you worry about the gap paid by your clients? How often do you exclude particular services from your practice (e.g., couples therapy) because there is no Medicare rebate attached?

I started private practice before there were any Medicare rebates available for psychological services. Colleagues of mine had full-time, profitable practices at the time. Without Medicare rebates. We need to bring our thinking back to that time and ask ourselves *"what other revenue streams am I ignoring outside of Medicare?"*

Now I want you to do the following journaling activity to unblock your thinking about what non-Medicare services you could be offering. You'll need a notebook, a really nice pen, somewhere comfortable to work, and a decent coffee, because this will take a while. (I would do this type of activity in a café, where decent coffee is on tap!)

JOURNALING ACTIVITY

Brainstorm as many psychological services as you can (e.g., couples counselling, individual therapy, coaching), including as many client populations as you can (e.g., older adults, children, executives), in as many formats as you can (e.g., group, mobile delivery, telephone, online). Try to fill a whole A4 page (more if you can). When you're done, draw a circle around each service, client population, and format that does NOT attract a Medicare rebate. Then I want you to list all the reasons stopping your practice from providing these services. Then I want you to write an A4 page on all the ways your practice COULD deliver these services. Finally, an A4 page on "my practice would be ….If we added …. service" for each of the new options you identified as possible contenders. When you've finished the above activity, write a list of all your contenders, and brainstorm how you might promote those services and who you would target your marketing towards (e.g., parenting skills groups promoted through the local school). Write as many ideas as you can for each of the non-Medicare options you identified. When you've done all that, research what others (e.g., counsellors, vocational rehabilitation providers, life coaches, and others charge for those services). This might involve spending some time on the phone pretending to be a potential client of these services. Don't worry, you won't go to hell!

Why did I ask you do this incredibly lengthy activity? Because you've just identified a paying caseload for a casual provisional psychologist while they work towards their full registration (with enough clients left over for a sub-contractor or two!). Congratulations!

CHAPTER 9

IMPOSTOR FEARS AND WHERE TO FIND THEM

The second biggest reason* (be honest, it's an excuse) that experienced clinicians give for not becoming Board Approved supervisors and taking on interns is lack of confidence. Well, they don't name it "lack of confidence", but they'll say things like: I want to get my clinical endorsement first, or I want to make sure I've got enough experience first, or I don't know if I know enough yet, or I haven't done enough supervisor training yet. Sound familiar? These excuses reflect a fear that the intern won't value what you have to offer as a supervisor.

*The number one excuse given by eligible supervisors in private practice is that they don't have time to supervise a student. I'm hoping we've smashed that myth by now.

Let's be really clear. Interns, provisionals, registrars all NEED supervision. They are dead keen to accrue the requisite hours to meet their minimum requirements. Your future supervisees will value your supervision (a) because they need it and (b) because by virtue of your being eligible to supervise, you have the requisite experience. As long as you are not acting outside your competencies (no, that does not mean "I don't feel ready"), or behaving inappropriately (no, you may not sleep with your supervisees), or drunk (save that for outside the supervision sessions), you are eligible and therefore able to supervise. And your supervisees will value your insights.

How do I know this? Because I, like you, have been a student intern and a registrar (of two APS colleges, aka glutton for punishment) and I remember how it felt to just need a supportive ear (and to accrue my hours!). I remember looking up to my supervisors and hoping they would have magical insights into my clinical dilemma du jour. And then I remember being a supervisor for the first time.

I made some terrible mistakes. I built walls around my "position" as supervisor, keeping boundaries strictly clear despite wanting so very much to connect personally and authentically with my supervisees. I don't know if my first supervisees will agree with this, but this is my recollection. I needed that wall to protect my own fears around not being taken seriously. I was afraid of not having all the answers all the time. I hid behind being a "grammar nazi" (their phrase) with their written work. And I felt an ivory tower would keep me safe from being exposed as a sham. Pfft! Bloody impostor fears!

But I Don't Think I Want To Supervise

If you don't want to supervise, that is perhaps a separate issue and I wonder then why you are reading this book? Perhaps try some journaling around this to unlock what is behind your lack of desire to mentor new clinicians. Did you have bad experiences? Do you fear being exposed as an imposter? Why is that? Who told you that you weren't good enough? If you've made it this far in your reading, I'd argue that you are at the very least curious about whether or not you could become a supervisor and build your team that way. If you think about supervision as leadership, as inspiration, as mentoring, as providing support and encouragement, NOT as being a font of all knowledge, you'll be on the right track in my books.

It took a long time for me to learn that there really is no such thing as perfect. If you believe that your supervisees expect that of you, and if you believe that you should know everything and have all the answers, you'll struggle. Because that is just not realistic or fair. Don't forget to be human. Ask yourself what your advice would be to your supervisee or your client. Why are you holding yourself to a higher, unattainable ideal?

Be up front about this with your supervisees too. Tell them that you don't know all the answers, and nobody can. Show them that they need to be realistic with themselves too. Remember your very first client? Remember the stress you felt, thinking that you should know what to do? Your supervisees are feeling that too. By demonstrating that none of us knows all of the answers all of the time, we give our supervisees permission to be real, and most importantly to know when to seek advice. Because they absolutely should know when to ask questions, and that it's okay to do so.

And guess what? It's okay for your supervisee to know more about a certain topic than you do. I still love to learn, and I'm very much open to learning from my supervisees. When supervisees feel that their knowledge and recent learning is valued, they will be motivated to contribute to your practice. And that's exactly how it should be.

And while we're on that topic, a word on millennials.

I went through uni before smart phones, before the internet was anywhere near as sophisticated as it is now. So yep, that means I had to slog my way through journals at the library to find the information I needed. That doesn't make my learning experience better or worse, just ancient! It breaks my heart to hear so many say things like "millennials are lazy" or "millennials are so entitled". I've certainly had clinicians on my team who have had a sense of entitlement that has left me startled (they are no longer with me, but that's a story for another day!). But there are personalities that can grate at any age and in every generation. The learning style and capacity of the digital generation is like nothing we've seen in previous generations. They work hard, but differently. They can see the world shrinking before their eyes. They aspire to be entrepreneurs and social media mavens. And that's okay. It's not narcissism and entitlement. It's motivation and passion manifest. If you start from a platform of letting your Gen-Millennial supervisees teach you what they know, while you're teaching them what you know, you'll have an amazing experience together. Why not let them encourage you to start a podcast, or some social media marketing for your practice? It's a brave new world, my friend!

Time for You

As a supervisor and the leader of your private practice team, even if it's still only a team of one, you have a lot on your plate. If you're running a private practice, congratulations on being a small business owner! It's so fulfilling to run your own show, see your name on the door, and be the boss of your domain. Of course, this also means the

How to Catch a Unicorn

responsibility for financial risk, tax obligations, insurances, administration and documentation all fall into your lap. It's exciting. It's daunting. And it's bloody stressful. As students of psychology, we are not taught at university how to be business owners. We were not taught to be team leaders. Or how to recruit. Or how to manage our finances. For some reason we expect that we will learn these things by osmosis. We expect that by hanging around long enough we'll somehow just pick it up. And some of us do. Well done to you if you fall into that category. But if you have no idea what you're doing and are scared to admit it, especially to your team, it's okay. We've all had moments (some longer than others) of being in that particular boat. But now is the time to stop it! Find a mentor, find a supervisor, find a support network. Being a practice owner and a leader can be incredibly isolating if you let it. Don't. Have a look on Facebook and you'll find a multitude of pages and groups dedicated to supporting mental health professionals. I have a mentor and I treasure the support and guidance I receive from her and those I've met through her. In fact, it was through her that I discovered that my knowledge around building a team with postgraduate students was of value to others. I had just assumed that everyone knew this stuff!

By participating in your own supervision or mentoring and by being comfortable talking about what you're learning from your own support networks, you're normalising the idea that ongoing supervision is valued. You'll reduce the risk of your own burnout and you'll be demonstrating to your team the importance of this for their own careers.

No matter how experienced you are, or how much of an expert you are in your field, you should find a supervisor or mentor who can support and guide you. Thanks to the wonders of the internet, if you need to look outside your local area for someone suitably skilled in your area to provide you with the support you need, you can. You can receive your supervision from anyone, anywhere in the world. What an amazing time to be flourishing in our profession!

It is by having the humility to accept guidance, and the wisdom to know you need it, that you will develop the quiet confidence you need to overcome your impostor fears, to take yourself out of your ivory tower of self-protection, and to thrive as a supervisor to your own supervisees.

How to Catch a Unicorn

CHAPTER 10

NEVER STOP ASKING QUESTIONS

My final words to you on being a great supervisor are simply this: Never stop asking questions. You're not a lecturer (well you might be, but not in this role), so you don't need to do all the talking. This is where your fear comes from: What if I don't know the answer? Forget the answer! Listen. And ask more questions. Empower your supervisee to find out their own answers if you can't figure it out between you.

Remember when you were a supervisee. Put yourself back in that time for a moment. Remember how it felt to have your supervisor ask you lots of questions. What did that feel like? If your supervisor came from a lofty authoritative space, those questions felt like interrogation, or criticism, or an assessment. Right? But if your supervisor came from a supportive and encouraging space, those questions felt more supportive. But I invite you to be more than supportive. Be CURIOUS! Be genuinely curious about how your supervisee is experiencing their work with their clients, how they are tolerating the stresses of dealing with risk issues, or how they are finding the time they need to learn, plan, and implement their work. Be genuinely curious about how they feel about their clients, how they feel about their journey from student to professional, and how they find working through treatment options. By being curious your supervisee will feel that you are interested, that you are partnering with them (rather than lecturing them), and they will feel supported because you are engaged.

And of course, being inquisitive keeps the conversation flowing without you having to feel that you need to know all the answers. By default you are encouraging reflective practice. If you need to reflect on this a little more, re-read Chapter 1 to revisit the impact this had one me.

Don't forget to spend some time reflecting on your experience of the supervision experience too. Both for yourself and for your supervisee. Wonder with an open mind and without judgement about how the relationship is going and what direction supervision is taking

Be inquisitive about all sorts of things to support your supervisee and yourself. Be inquisitive about technologies that help you communicate more effectively. Be inquisitive about developments within the profession. Be inquisitive about your own learning needs. This will open you up to accepting peer support, mentoring, supervision, and ongoing training for yourself, which in turn keeps you fresh and relevant in the eyes of your supervisees (and a great role model for how to engage in ongoing professional development).

How to Catch a Unicorn

HOW TO FIND YOUR QUIET CONFIDENCE

You've made it to the end of the book. Thank you for taking this time out of your busy world to walk through these ideas with me. You've been great company! I hope that by considering some of the concepts and reflections that I've shared with you here you will now be in a better place to tap into that inner warmth and curiosity that make you such a great clinician. You'll now be able to translate that into your roadmap to becoming a great supervisor.

Your take home message is that you don't have anything to prove. And this means you have nothing to fear. You are fully trained, fully qualified, and have enough experience to be an eligible supervisor. By taking on a supervisee in your practice you can provide great opportunities for learning and you can build your team. Win win! Don't let the fear of not being "good enough" stop you from exploring this great opportunity to support the profession and support the growth of your team.

Remember, you are not required to know everything, to have seen everything, or to have treated everything. The things you don't know will help your supervisees as much as the things you do know, because this will provide opportunities for you and your supervisee to learn something together. Even better, it will provide opportunities for your supervisees to teach you something. Can't get better learning than that!

By taking time to trust yourself and trust your knowledge base, by trusting that supervisees need supervision and are ready and waiting for you to work with them, and by trusting that you have so much more to offer than you give yourself credit for, you can step into your role as a calm, reflective, inquisitive, supportive supervisor. Your quiet confidence will blossom gently and fully before your eyes.

WHO IS TESS CRAWLEY?

Ancient History ...

Tess is an Australian psychologist, supervisor, mentor, podcaster and writer. She has been a registered psychologist since 2001 and completed her PhD in clinical psychology in 2004. She holds AHPRA-endorsement in both Clinical and Forensic Psychology, and is a Board-Approved Supervisor. Tess is a former psychology lecturer, research supervisor, and University Psychology Clinic Director. She was one of the original trainers in Medicare Australia's Better Access when this initiative was released in 2006. Tess has also worked in adult community mental health, vocational rehabilitation, and forensic mental health (within both the Tasmanian and Queensland prison services). Before all this, Tess was an actor and photographer!

Private Practice ...

Tess started a solo private practice in 2001, branching into a group practice model in 2009. She is the Director of Dr Tess Crawley & Associates, a large Tasmanian group private practice with offices in Hobart and Launceston and a team of over 20 clinicians and admin staff. The practice has two subsidiary arms: Hobart Perinatal Psychology and Rural Psychology Tasmania, reflecting two of the special interest areas of her team. In her clinical practice, Tess focusses on clinical and forensic work within the perinatal field.

Quiet Confidence ...

Over the years, Tess has supervised or mentored over 100 students, registrars, and experienced clinicians. Since 2017 she has focussed on her passion area of mentoring mental health professionals through her mentoring programs, Quiet Confidence. She provides support and content via Facebook groups and pages, as well as tailored mentoring programs, retreats, workshops, and written resources.

Contact Tess via her website or through Facebook if you would like more information on her mentoring and training programs.

 www.tesscrawley.com.au

 dr.tess.crawley.psychology

 @TessCrawley

 Search for Tess Crawley and Quiet Confidence under pages and groups and say hello!